PEACE IN *His* PRESENCE

An Excessively Blessed Devotional

DR. HALENE GIDDENS

An Excessively Blessed Devotional
Peace In His Presence

Printed in the U.S.A.

ISBN: 978-1-7321277-4-6

FOR MORE INFORMATION CONTACT:
760-951-8500
www.destinychristiancenter.org

Cover Art: Abraham's Ink Publishing House

Acknowledgements

I'm so honored once again to dedicate this devotional to my God: You are so mindful of each of us and desire to inspire us for our great success stories. Through Your Leading and Guidance, I'm grateful that You allowed me to add this small contribution alongside many faith-building tools.

To my beloved spouse, mentor, motivator, and holy man of God: I'm thankful to God for your leadership, friendship, and unconditional love.

To my beautiful children: May you abound in God's righteousness and receive His Amazing Grace.

To my gracious Mom: I love you forever.

To my Mother-in-love and Sister-in-love: May you abound in God's unfailing favor over your lives.

To my godchildren and spiritual children in the faith: Your love overwhelms me. I pray only the choicest of God's blessings be released over your lives.

To my DCC and DIMA family: I hope you know what jewels you are to Bishop Giddens and me. My heart's desire is that you would abound in the blessings of the Lord, lacking in no good thing!

Be Excessively Blessed!

A NOTE FROM *Dr. Halene*

Hi! I'm so blessed that you would make the choice to open this devotional *Peace In His Presence* and peruse the content written inside. May you be richly increased because of it, or as I constantly like to say, "May you be Excessively Blessed!"

As you continue to develop in the knowledge of our Lord and Savior Jesus Christ, I pray these short teachings will be another tool for you to achieve that aim.

We can't live this good life without Him. So, we might as well learn more about Him.

This devotional is the second installment of a three-part series based on our time during a worldwide pandemic. We were shut down for about two years, unable to gather together as family, friends, coworkers, and as a body of believers. And we're all still trying to navigate through this new normal. Yet, I believe hearts were moved across America and worldwide to find ways to encounter God. Perhaps not every Christian Believer, but many were on a quest to know Him more.

In such a stressful time we're living in, I wanted to do my part to encourage God's people to find comfort and peace by hearing His Word—the premise of this devotional.

To find God's Promises through experiencing His Word is the ultimate place of peace for you and me. His Word never fails; it has all power and will work in our lives when we apply it and then take time to allow it to do its work in us.

When we hear the Word and read the Word, we believe the Word and receive the Word with thanksgiving. Our faith is in action, and this is how the Word works. His Word is good for our souls, medicine for our minds, and a healing balm for our hearts.

Let me write it again. His Word never fails. Although we may fail and fall short, we may miss it and mess up; God's Compelling Word brings us right back to Him.

The idea of this devotional is to seek a life of dedication and consecration towards our God. Reading, comprehending, and spending time with God in prayer brings a devotedness to Him. To have a time of devotion, it must become a part of our habitual deeds—something we can't live without—by making the Word a necessary part of our lives.

I believe our Heavenly Father wants to be our necessity and Daily Bread. Therefore, when we hunger and thirst after the righteousness found in knowing Christ, we are filled and fulfilled.

Everything in this world seems designed to take us away from knowing God for ourselves. The enemy of our souls doesn't mind us knowing something about God in the abstract, on the fringes of our consciousness. He doesn't even care if we attend church regularly, just as long as we don't become fully engaged in the worship experience. Engaging in Him means being fully involved in hearing and receiving the Word of God.

But having an authentic and intimate relationship with a Holy and Awesome God is a different story. This devotional and other Christ-centered writings are designed to draw you closer to God. I pray that the time you spend reading your devotional causes you to reflect and be refreshed in God's Holy Word as you get to know Him more.

Oh, and by the way, in my writings, I like to take certain liberties in diction, if you would. For example, I like to use capital letters in reference to God's characteristics and qualities. I may even draw out sentences, causing them to be a bit lengthy in thought and theme. This may or may not align with grammatical correctness, but I like to bring a little punch to the point I'm determined to make with the help of the Holy Spirit.

I pray you enjoy partaking in this devotional this month and in the coming months. And as you take the time to *Pause in His Presence,* I pray you find great *Peace in His Presence,* and again you would be *Excessively Blessed*!

ONE

Peace in His Presence

Let the peace of Christ [the inner calm of one who walks daily with Him] be the controlling factor in your hearts [deciding and settling questions that arise]. To this peace indeed you were called as members in one body [of believers]. And be thankful [to God always].

COLOSSIANS 3:15 AMP

My prayer for you today is that the Peace of God surrounds your heart and your mind. May you be governed and guided by God's Peace and His Wisdom for whatever task that may arise today. Finally, I pray you have an amazing day, and you would choose to rejoice and be glad today and every day.

The Peace of God is one of God's wonderful gifts for each one of us. When we receive Jesus Christ as our Lord and Savior, immediately peace comes to comfort our hearts and minds. There's a joy that awakens us to this new life of love we get to experience with our Holy God. If you have not experienced the joy of the Lord lately, this is a good time to embrace God's Peace that fills us with His Joy. Sometimes it takes just a moment to *Pause in His Presence* and then receive His Peace. It can transform each day which in turn can transform your life.

Your Savior does not want you to be without His Peace. The Amplified Version of this Scripture says the Peace of Christ is an "inner calm." This "inner calm" is only present when we make the choice to walk daily with Christ. I always like to emphasize that walking with the Lord is a choice that we must make daily. Some may believe that making a fresh commitment to Jesus isn't necessary every single day, yet it most definitely is!

Proverbs 3:5 in the Amplified Version says, "Trust in and rely confidently on the Lord with all of your heart and do not rely on your own insight or understanding." That reads like something needing to take place every single day! Not just in the hardest of times, but in all of your times and "In all your ways," verse 6 says, "know and acknowledge and recognize Him...."

Acknowledging and recognizing your Sovereign Savior as Lord over your life brings about this "inner calm" and peace that only comes from intimately knowing Him. The Scripture says to let this peace be the controlling factor in your hearts. This peace decides and settles all the questions that arise in your heart and mind.

Did you know that every question we have is settled when we receive the peace Christ died to give us? This doesn't necessarily mean that we will have the answer to every question. Instead, it means we will enjoy His calming and settling peace amid the barrage of questions and concerns.

When you read Colossians 3:1 in the Amplified Bible, it admonishes us to "keep seeking the things above, where Christ is, seated at the right hand of God." It continues to say, "set your mind and keep focused habitually on the things above [the heavenly things]…."

It takes real effort to not focus on the things that happen around us and to us. According to Colossians 3:3, we can do this because our lives are dead to this world and have been made alive, anew, and hidden in Christ Jesus. Although we're no longer of this world, we still live in this world, and the things in this world affect all of us.

And that's just it! We must take the time to make the time to center our lives around Christ and His Word. Christ's Gift of Peace as your center and circumference is the only way to get through your day. Confess His Word, announce His Word, and speak His Word daily. You can have peace during the most horrific storms when you stay in the Love of God.

Shout His Word from the rooftops if the world is bombarding your thoughts, taking you away from God's Presence of Peace. Stay planted, rooted, and stable in the Word of God. Invite the Presence of God right in the space where you are and experience the Peace of God by being thankful to your God. Real peace is found in His Presence.

My Notes

TWO

The Perfect Teachings of the Lord

The Lord's teachings are perfect. They give strength to his people. The Lord's rules can be trusted. They help even the foolish become wise. The Lord's laws are right. They make people happy. The Lord's commands are good. They show people the right way to live.

His teachings are worth more than gold. They are sweeter than the best honey dripping from the honeycomb.

May my words and thoughts please you. Lord, you are my Rock—the one who rescues me.

Psalm 19:7-8, 10, 14 ESV

God bless you today! I pray that as you seek the Lord in His Word, you find that His Word is sweet to your soul. As you lift up your eyes to Him, I pray you rest in His Assurance that He is the Light to your day and will illuminate your path.

This Psalm of David happens to be one of my favorites. Verses 7-9 have a certain rhythm and cadence about them centered on the blessing of the Word of God, especially when read in the King James Version. According to verse 10, the Word of the Lord is worth more to us than pure gold; it's sweeter than honey straight from the honeycomb, and you know how sweet honey can be. We need to embrace the Word of God for our everyday lives with this type of hunger, desire, and necessity. It's a benefit for our physical, emotional, and spiritual health.

Verse 12 of this chapter goes on to say that people cannot see their own mistakes, "So don't let me commit secret sins." I love how the psalmist freely shares his inner thoughts about himself, revealing that we can have sin issues that may be a secret to others, but not to our God! Verse 13 gets down to the heart of the matter and says, "Don't let me do what I know is wrong… if you help me, I can be pure and free from sin." Open and honest dialogue with our Heavenly Father is liberating and causes us to have an unrestrained relationship with Him. He knows us anyway, so we might as well come completely clean with Him.

There is hope, help, and health as we lend our lives to the Lord and allow His Word to have first place in our hearts. When we acknowledge the Lord's Teachings are perfect, and we continue to adhere to His Commandments, we are changed! We have the privilege to live the sweet life with the One we say we love. God's Laws are not to keep us bound or blocked from enjoying life but for our betterment to have peace in this life. We keep them close, so we won't suffer the consequences of negative choices. Although twists and turns can hit our lives unexpectedly, we can realign with God's Divine Word and become centered even in our worst storms.

His Teachings are perfect. You don't need to add anything to them or take anything away from them, so don't do it! His Word gives you strength. His Rules can be trusted. They even help the foolish (which can be you and me in any given season) become wise.

Receive these words today and allow them to penetrate your heart. Place the Word as a priority over your life, just as the psalmist declared in this song. Know that the Lord has given you every single day to live a joyful, wisdom-filled life.

Let the sweetness of God's Word cause you to be completely up close and honest with Him. Let Him hear about your deepest inner thoughts. Then allow Him to heal those areas in your life that may not be in line with His Word. Give Him every issue, every pain, and every secret today. Allow Him to help you so that your words and thoughts may be pleasing to Him. He is your Rock—the One Who will always rescue you! Then you can continue to rejoice in each and every day He has given you!

My Notes

THREE

Wisdom's Generosity

And if anyone longs to be wise, ask God for wisdom and he will give it! He won't see your lack of wisdom as an opportunity to scold you over your failures, but he will overwhelm your failures with his generous grace. Just make sure you ask empowered by confident faith without doubting you will receive.

James 1:5-6a TPT

Hi! How are you today? I pray you are abiding in God's Love at this moment. I pray you find yourself longing to know more about Him, wanting to listen to His voice. Most importantly, I pray you seek God's Wisdom for your life. Yes, you can operate in God's Infinite Wisdom every day. My hope for you today is you would allow the Holy Spirit to remind you that your days are secure in Him.

This world's measure of wisdom is finite. It's mainly limited to what can be seen, touched, and heard; it's psychological, sometimes physiological. However, God's Wisdom knows no bounds; it encompasses all aspects of our natural and spiritual lives. Moreover, His Wisdom is timeless and is free for the asking. Our Father longs for His children to simply ask for His Insight. After all, He knows your beginning and end; there is no One better to go to than the One Who created you.

James, the brother of Jesus, whose name translated from the Hebrew Jacob to the Greek pronunciation James, points out this truth in his letter to the Jews. As we face difficulties, and we will, we are to see them as invaluable opportunities to employ the Wisdom of God. It's called the testing and trying of our faith. I know this may seem almost impossible to do–stirring the power within us to be able to endure tough experiences. Yet, the Spirit of God in us most definitely helps us!

As our endurance strengthens, perfection is released unto us, leaving nothing missing or lacking. The key is to have His Mind and Thoughts concerning every area of our lives. This is absolutely wonderful! We can operate every day tapping into the Mind of Christ! We cannot face tests alone and expect to pass. Instead, the Holy Spirit living within us Helps us win the battles that come against us!

This requires God's Wisdom. Our God will not scold or get angry with us for our failures, for the Word promises He will overwhelm our failures with His Generous Grace. When we ask for Wisdom, empowered by confident faith, we must believe that we receive it. We can't be undecided or unbelieving; this leaves us unstable and unable to obtain anything from our Heavenly Father.

James lived with Jesus. He walked with Him, listened to His Teachings, and saw how God's Only Begotten Son gave gifts generously. Jesus healed the sick, fed the hungry, lifted the heads of those in pain, and raised the dead. James saw Wisdom walk this earth and how open God is willing to share His Gifts with us. Yet, we cannot rely only on our natural understanding when it comes to important decisions that need to be made in our lives.

God will always lead us to Wisdom when we really desire to receive it. This Wisdom can come directly from the Inner Witness, Who is the Holy Spirit, or from God Who leads us to wise people filled with wisdom, knowledge, and understanding.

When we trust the Holy Spirit within us to bring us through every difficulty, when we trust that God has given us the wisdom we've asked for, and when we pray His Will be done in every detail of this life He created us to live, we will experience the Manifold Blessings of God. He is always willing to give us just what we need right when we need it!

God gives Wisdom through prayer, people, preparation, and even problems. Acknowledging that you need His Help to maneuver through every day is wisdom. So, I pray that you accept His Generous Gift for your entire well-being.

Talk to Him, stay in His Presence, listen for His Response, and allow God to lead you to Wisdom. Expect to receive Wisdom in every decision you make on this beautiful day! Receive God's Wisdom and walk in God's Peace. God bless you!

My Notes

FOUR

The Royal Law of Love Shows No Prejudice

My dear brothers and sisters, fellow believers in our glorious Lord Jesus Christ— how could we say that we have faith in him and yet favor one group of people above another?

Your calling is to fulfill the royal law of love as given to us in this Scripture: "You must love and value your neighbor as you love and value yourself!" For keeping this law is the noble way to live. But when you show prejudice you commit sin and you violate this royal law of love!

JAMES 2:1, 8-9 TPT

Good morning, good afternoon, or good evening! I sure hope it's good no matter what part of the day it is for you! I pray that you would open your heart expecting Christ's Over-Abundant Love for you! As you may know, God is Love; His Love sent His Son to die for our sins. In a world filled with deceit, pride, hatred, and lust, unconditional love can seem like a foreign concept for most people. Yet, as believers, this love is the precious gift we receive and then show to the world.

I want to encourage you today, God's chosen and beloved, to love and value who God created you to be. You are made in His Image and Likeness. You have been made precious in His Sight. You become more like Him in your actions as you observe His Ways through His Word and seek His Presence. Our lives are a living reflection of Christ's Love and Light. Therefore, we should openly allow His Abundance to flow through us.

The above passage of the Bible reminds us that we are royalty. Our Father is the King of kings, and His entire Persona is Love. Love is the foundation of the Kingdom of God. We have been invited and welcomed into God's Royal Kingdom of Love. His first Commandment to us is to love. With everything in us, we should love the Lord our God with all our heart, mind, and strength. His second Royal Decree is to love our neighbor as we love ourselves. So, we are to love and value God, love and value ourselves, and then we can love and value everybody else. James tells us that to love is a law that we must abide by. This law excludes all prejudice.

There is no favoritism in God's Kingdom. He has accepted both Jew and Gentile, rich and poor, as His Own, and because

He has, we should as well. If we show prejudice because someone is different, we violate the Sacred Law of God. We need to be careful of our actions and look through His Eyes of Love. We should make every effort to be sensitive to the Holy Spirit's Leading and mirror the love that our Father displays. There is no partiality in the Love of God.

Walk in your royal calling of love today as a son or daughter of the King. Value who you are and Whose you are. Your Father is Love. Let there be no preferential treatment when offering out this most beautiful gift. Remember how this same gift was so unreservedly given to you. His Love knows no boundaries, so you don't have to be bound either. You can freely give this gift of love as Your Heavenly Father leads you to do so. You are valuable, and you are loved. Always remember this truth! Share this truth with others around you today as you are a reflection of God's unconditional Love. God bless you and I love you!

My Notes

FIVE

Joy in Purpose

...let us keep on running in the way which is marked out for us, Having our eyes fixed on Jesus, the guide and end of our faith, who went through the pains of the cross, not caring for the shame, because of the joy which was before him, and who has now taken his place at the right hand of God's seat of power.

Hebrews 12:1c-2 BBE

This is a wonderful day to be alive, and because you are, there is still so much for you to fulfill, and a destiny for you to walk in! Because He has a purpose for you, Jesus desires to guide you with the Leading of His Holy Spirit in and through it all. As you welcome the gift of this day, make it your delight to walk in His Presence, fulfilling His Joy that He has for you.

Hebrews chapter 12 brings such hope to the believer. We are told in the first verse that a great cloud of witnesses surrounds us. So many have gone before us, setting an example of how we can boldly live this Christian life. When we put all our expectations in the Guide and End of our faith—the Author and Finisher of our faith—we can run this race with patience, knowing He will fulfill His Promises to us.

We may face numerous trials in this lifetime and be met with some burdens along the way. However, if we keep looking to Jesus, He Who now sits at the Right Hand of God's Seat of Power, we can still have victory even in the hard times. When we keep our thoughts on what He physically went through to pay a debt we could never pay, we receive strength to continue this walk with Him and live this life according to His Will and Desire, not our own.

Jesus wants a relationship with us. He could endure all He suffered because He knew the prize was worth it. We are that prize! You are His prize! He knew that the pain and agony He endured would be to save all of humanity. Our destiny now is to focus on the joy before us and live an Excessively Blessed life in His Presence. It's a daily choice to choose to be Excessively Blessed. Jesus died so that we can live it out on this side of

Heaven. The blessed life is not based on our feelings or outer circumstances. It's an inner knowing and an acknowledgment of our Savior's overwhelming Love for us.

I pray you choose to follow after God's Calling on your life. I pray that if you feel weary or weak, you fix your eyes on Him and gain the strength and power you need for your life. Follow the examples of those who have gone before, believing your Father will answer your every need. He wants to help you; He wants to use you. Walk in the authority He has given you today! Let Him be the Guide and End of your faith. I love you and pray His choicest Blessings are yours! There is so much joy in your purpose!

My Notes

SIX

Don't Let the Wounds Hinder Your Way

Let the peace of Christ [the inner calm of one who walks daily with Him] be the controlling factor in your hearts [deciding and settling questions that arise]. To this peace indeed you were called as members in one body [of believers]. And be thankful [to God always].

Hebrews 12:1,2 TPT

Praise the Lord, amazing child of God! I pray you're Excessively Blessed today! In the previous devotion we looked at Hebrews chapter 12 from the Bible in Basic English Version, but today I'd like to share it from the Passion Translation. I pray this different version is an encouragement to you as the Word of God should be. Every time we have the opportunity to be in the Word of God, we infuse our lives with health and healing. The Word is a healing balm. So, I pray that as you read it today, you will be healed on the inside and walk in health on the outside.

No matter what you're facing today, don't allow the wounds that you may have endured nor the sins of your past or present keep you from going forward with your God! We know wounds, physical and emotional, can leave heavy scars that may be difficult to heal or get over. These wounds may cause us to stumble around in our lives because of the severe pain they've left behind. Wounds can sometimes feel permanent or resurface in the worst of times. In the Passion Translation, the Word of the Living God encourages us to let go of the wounds that have pierced us along with the sin that we can so easily fall into. I'd like to put a reminder here that this letter is written to believers!

The Scripture goes on to say that when we leave our negative past in the past along with the sin issues that try to hold us hostage, we can run this marathon called life with passion and determination! We are able and equipped to run long and run strong because the pathway has already been prepared for us. It's already been marked out and mapped out for us to win! Jesus is at the finish line cheering us on! He's right there with you every time your foot hits the pavement. He wants us to win!

He's saying, "Just look at my wounds and look at my scars. I did this for you so you can endure to the end." I know you know this already: He's right there when you lay down and when you get up. He's always ready to encourage you to go in the direction He has prepared for you.

You've got a whole bunch of people who have gone before you who have already run and completed their race, and it's in you to complete your race as well. Don't let anything stop you! Especially not your past or present circumstances!

Allow the wounds that have afflicted you to begin to heal; don't allow them to fester or worsen. Instead, allow Jesus to be your Healing Balm. Let the Healing Salve of His Anointed Blood wash your wounds, heal your heart, and bury your sin. He'll do that if you let Him. Every time that wound wants to start hurting, look to Jesus. When the sin issue wants to rear its ugly head, look to Jesus. Keep looking up to Him, and don't look back! Your faith in Jesus is the factor that gets you to the finish line!

My Notes

SEVEN

Evidence of God's Faithful Love

For the Lord's training of your life is the evidence of his faithful love. And when he draws you to himself, it proves you are his delightful child. Fully embrace God's correction as part of your training, for he is doing what any loving father does for his children. For who has ever heard of a child who never had to be corrected? We all should welcome God's discipline as the validation of authentic sonship. For if we have never once endured his correction it only proves we are strangers and not sons.

HEBREWS 12:6-8 TPT

Praise the Lord, and God bless you today! I pray you're doing well. I want to share again from Hebrews chapter 12 in The Passion Translation, but a few verses down. The book of Hebrews is a letter to the Jewish people to let them know Jesus is better. The author wanted to prove that by receiving Jesus and knowing Him personally is so much better than hiding behind the blood sacrifices of lambs, goats and other animals. Jesus' Sacrifice is better. His Blood saves, heals, and sets us free. No matter how bloody and gory those animal sacrifices became, nothing beats what Jesus did on the cross for you and me. This thought is woven throughout the book of Hebrews.

It seems that the writer deviates from exhorting to "not despise the chastening of the Lord" (King James Version). He goes on to say "for whom the Lord loves He chastises." The Passion Translation calls it training for your life. Either way, it doesn't feel good when the Lord has to correct us. It especially doesn't feel good when He uses specific people to do it. But if we truly belong to Him and want to mature as sons and daughters of the Father, then we will receive the "scourging," which is simply a good spanking from our God. A real son and daughter want correction, direction, and instruction. You shouldn't want to be out here on your own trying to figure it out by yourself.

When we insist on going our own way, we pay our own fare like Jonah did when he went down into the belly of the whale. That for sure was a sticky situation Jonah had gotten himself into! Yet, God caused that fish, according to Jonah's book, to spit him out right where God wanted him the entire time! When God's Hand is in your life, you just gotta do what He's Leading you to do! It's so much better when we simply follow His Lead.

It's so much better than just doing any old thing and hoping it all works out.

We need the training, we need the correction, and sometimes we even need the spanking. This is what maturity is all about; this is what growing up in God is all about, when we can receive the Discipline from the Lord with patience. When we get out of line or cross it, we need God's Hand over our lives to help us get back in line to walk the line He has for us.

The Word of God says we are to "fully embrace God's correction as a part of our training." This particular translation goes on to say that our Heavenly Father is doing what any loving father does for his children. But unfortunately, so many people, young and old, do not want to be told what to do. Although God allows us to make decisions independently, good or bad, many people would rather figure it all out on their own.

Sometimes, this can make us feel like we are on our own, all alone, trying to figure it out.

God wants to lead and guide you into the "green pastures" He has for you. And sometimes, it takes correction and discipline to get you there. So, don't run from the chastening of the Lord. He loves you dearly and desires only the very best for your life. And never forget this: Daddy always knows best!

My Notes

EIGHT

Yahweh: Our Guardian God!

I look up to the mountains and hills, longing for God's help. But then I realize that our true help and protection is only from the Lord, our Creator who made the heavens and the earth. He will guard and guide me, never letting me stumble or fall. God is my keeper; he will never forget nor ignore me. He will never slumber nor sleep; he is the Guardian-God for his people, Israel.

Yahweh himself will watch over you; he's always at your side to shelter you safely in his presence.

Psalm 121:1-5 TPT

Hey! Praises be unto the Living God of Hope and Peace! May you continue to look up with expectancy towards our God. Never look down with complacency because up is where your help and your hope is going to always come from.

Psalm 121 is one of the Songs of Ascents, sacred songs sung by the people of God as they traveled up to Jerusalem to worship and bring their sacrifices to the Lord at least three times a year. They would look up into the hills or mountains as they went on their journey and sing these songs of worship and praise to their God.

The Lord our Creator desires for you to look up to Him every single day, whether you're in trouble or your day is ordinary. In actuality, there are no ordinary days when you take the time to look up to God first as your Source for direction, comfort, and care. He's always right there, willing and wanting to answer your prayer because He wants your life to be extraordinary.

Now, don't look around for the extraordinary to appear like a shiny new toy. Material things can manifest, but it's not the end-all of what God can or desires to do in you. Sometimes, it's the minute and seemingly tiny things that may look small to others that can be exceptional in your life. For instance, the extraordinary can be the whisper of God's Word specifically for you or a small token of His Presence and Love that can illuminate your day. It can be the very thing you need to hear, see, or experience that is tailor-made just for your pleasure, enjoyment, necessity, or reassurance.

Yahweh, one of many Names of God, means Self Existent;

this Name also means Beacon in the Hebrew. A *beacon* is *a guiding or warning light or that which is in an elevated place seeing near, far, and above!* He is our Light in the darkness.

The Jewish people humbly spoke the Name of the Lord because of their reverence for Him. So much so that they barely wanted to breathe His Name from their lips because they felt it was too Holy to even pronounce.

Yet, this Holy God, Eternal Jehovah, cared so much for them that He kept and protected them every day. He's still the same God with all Power and Might. He has not lost His Authority, and He's still the One Who's keeping watch over you. So, you can rest in His Care; He's not going anywhere, and He's not going to sleep on you, ever. He will protect you now, and He will protect you forevermore. He's got you and everything and everyone that concerns you. So don't look around and don't look down; always look up.

My Notes

NINE

Overflow With Joy

Be cheerful with joyous celebration in every season of life. Let your joy overflow! And let gentleness be seen in every relationship, for our Lord is ever near. Don't be pulled in different directions or worried about a thing. Be saturated in prayer throughout each day, offering your faith-filled requests before God with overflowing gratitude. Tell him every detail of your life, then God's wonderful peace that transcends human understanding, will guard your heart and mind through Jesus Christ.

PHILIPPIANS 4:4-7 TPT

God bless you today! You have been Handcrafted by the Lord, Homemade in Heaven, Perfectly Placed on Earth for this season of time to be everything our Heavenly Father has created you to be. I just wanted to remind you of that very important fact!

I pray that you are doing well today. Whatever your circumstances are, whatever you're facing, I pray you will continue to focus on your Heavenly Father, Who's got you. Sometimes, it seems like something different hits us on a daily basis. Just be reassured that Jesus will always have you. Therefore, whatever your cares, let Him handle them because He will. He'll give you the Wisdom and Help to handle every problem. He has the resources just for you. He has the person, the plan, and the program already designed to give you what you need. Always make sure to keep your God as your priority.

The Word of God in Philippians 4:4 encourages us to "Be cheerful with joyous celebration in every season of your life." It then adds more to it by declaring, "Let your joy overflow!" The Amplified Classic Version states, "Rejoice in the Lord always [delight, gladden yourselves in Him]; again I say, Rejoice!" The Apostle Paul is not asking us to rejoice, nor is he saying to be cheerful based on our feelings. Instead, he wrote this as a command to just do it in every season, for any reason, no matter what's going on around you. Even though you may not be able to think of a single reason to be full of joy, be glad in the Lord anyway!

And that's the point. Our gladness and our joy are centered in the Lord and nothing else. Gladness and joy keep us centered and not pulled in so many directions with so many distractions. He makes us glad not by superficial exterior things but by coming to know Him more. We can be gracious to those around us because the Joy of the Lord keeps our hearts and minds. At all times, He's consistently close to us, especially when we celebrate Him with joy. We can come to Him with faith-filled prayers, expecting to receive the answers we need because we allow joy to be full in us.

I love how The Passion Translation writes that we should "Be saturated in prayer throughout each day." Being saturated means to be completely immersed and engulfed, meaning we are covered head to toe in prayers of thanksgiving and gratitude! How can we do that? By being thankful all day, every day, continuously praying and thanking Him for answers throughout the day. While sitting on your laptop for school or work, be thankful. When washing the clothes and cleaning your space, be thankful. Cooking meals or taking out the trash, be thankful. Even if you're immobile, take a moment to lift your hands, if you can, and be thankful. That's how you stay saturated. Allow God's Wonderful Peace to cover your heart and mind to fill you with His Peace. His Word Works.

My Notes

TEN

Godly Character with God's Gift of Grace

So I, the prisoner for the Lord, appeal to you to live a life worthy of the calling to which you have been called [that is, to live a life that exhibits godly character, moral courage, personal integrity, and mature behavior—a life that expresses gratitude to God for your salvation], with all humility [forsaking self-righteousness], and gentleness [maintaining self-control], with patience, bearing with one another in [unselfish] love.

Yet grace [God's undeserved favor] was given to each one of us [not indiscriminately, but in different ways] in proportion to the measure of Christ's [rich and abundant] gift.

Ephesians 4:1-2, 7 AMP

God bless you and praises be unto our Most High God. May God's Ever-Abounding Grace and Favor manifest in your life until it overflows. May you experience the Favor of God today as you go throughout your day, employing godly conduct. His Grace will be given to you in abundant supply because He loves you just that much.

Looking at our Scripture verses today, I love how Paul calls himself a prisoner of the Lord instead of a prisoner of his circumstances. Paul, as we know, was placed under house arrest for turning the world, at that time, "upside down" by sharing the Gospel of Jesus Christ. Although he was condemned for exhibiting godly character and preaching righteousness, he still encouraged others to do all that they could to live upright lives before God.

Everyone is called by God to live this beautiful life of faith and trust in God. We can live godly lives exhibiting godly character, moral courage, personal integrity, and mature behavior. How are we able to do this? We can live this way with God's Help, Grace and Favor. Simply stated, we can live right when those around us may be living wrong; that's moral courage.

Because we have been created on purpose for purpose, we need our Heavenly Father's Gift of Abundant Grace to help us fulfill His Will on this side of Heaven. Sometimes, we don't always feel like exhibiting the Character of Christ every single day or every single moment of our day. In those times we have to shake ourselves, and just like Cher said to Nicolas Cage in the 1987 movie Moonstruck, "Snap out of it!" When you snap out of yourself and remind yourself of who you are, you can call on your godly character and handle the situations thrown your way.

Godly character and conduct are a choice. We can choose to operate out of our own emotions or feelings, or we can take a moment to breathe in deep and announce to ourselves: "I have God's Gift of Grace to deal with my current state of affairs." His Grace can keep our hearts, minds, and emotions. His Grace allows us to handle our doubts, our losses, and our fears. His Grace truly is sufficient for us (2 Corinthians 12:9).

The word *sufficient* in our English definitions means *adequate* or *enough*. It also means *plenty of, ample supply and abundant.* In Greek, it carries the connotation "to raise a barrier." We can rise above our current state of affairs when we take on the Character of Christ and allow God's Amazing Grace to keep our hearts and minds. Coincidentally, this causes us to respond better throughout our day.

In the middle of your situation, God's Grace will cause you to employ godly character, which helps produce the Abundance of God's Favor over your life. As you reread today's Scriptures, ask the Holy Spirit to help you take on these beautiful character attributes!

My Notes

ELEVEN

We Need Each Other

And he has generously given each one of us supernatural grace, according to the size of the gift of Christ.

And he has appointed some with grace to be apostles, and some with grace to be prophets, and some with grace to be evangelists, and some with grace to be pastors, and some with grace to be teachers. And their calling is to nurture and prepare all the holy believers to do their own works of ministry, and as they do this they will enlarge and build up the body of Christ.

Ephesians 4:7, 11-12 TPT

While sitting at my desk in my home office today, I read this quote: "Don't worry about tomorrow; God is already there." Your Father has tomorrow already prepared for you. Even if your days are especially difficult, your God will be right there in the trenches with you. He's ultimately the best battle buddy on the planet.

Today's verse in the book of Ephesians states that each one of us has generously been given supernatural grace by Christ. Christ means "Anointed" and in Greek, it's the word "Christos" or "Christ the Messiah." The Name Christ also means "to smear" and "to be rubbed with oil." God's Gift of Grace is the anointing smeared over our lives to be a help to others in honor to our God.

Some of us may remember being rubbed down with lotion or oil by our mothers or caregivers, or we've used this routine with our own children. Almost every part of the body was smeared with oil, leaving no dry areas on the skin.

Completing this treatment everyday causes our skin to be clean, supple, pliable, and bendable without cracking and hurting, which can cause bleeding. With this application of oil, our skin can endure the harsh temperatures of the sun, cold wind, and any outdoor activities. It isn't just about the skin looking good but also feeling good. It is also necessary for the health of the skin. It seems like a tedious job to be oiled from head to toe, yet it's beneficial to the one who follows this regimen.

The anointing on our lives, which is the grace on our lives, has been given to us by Christ the Anointed One for our benefit to succeed in this life. We need God's Grace daily to thrive, flourish, and advance. The anointing oil has been smeared on your life to protect you as well as to benefit others. Receive this oil daily.

Your life adds value to others just by you being the best you that God gifted you to be. It's the very reason we are here; at least that's a major part. We must continually give our lives to the Lord so He can pour His life in us to pour out on others. In a very significant way, the Grace Gift that God has placed on your life is to be a beautiful help to the Body of Christ, His Believers, and His Church.

As depicted in the above verse in the King James Version, our God gave the fivefold ministry for "the perfecting of the saints." These gifts, which work through men and women of God, are given to us from the Lord. Their purpose is to equip, strengthen, and complete us so we can live and share the Good News of the Gospel.

Receive your gifts! First, receive the Grace Giftings of those individuals Anointed by God to preach faith to you. Then, accept the Grace Gift on your life to be everything you need to be to do ministry work: simply serving others. The Body of Christ needs your gift. When we work together, we grow higher and do so much better. Receive the full measure of God's Gift of Grace in your life today! Just lift your hands and say, "I receive!"

My Notes

TWELVE

The Glorious Inner Strength You Need to Succeed

I ask him to strengthen you by his Spirit—not a brute strength but a glorious inner strength— that Christ will live in you as you open the door and invite him in. And I ask him that with both feet planted firmly on love, you'll be able to take in with all followers of Jesus the extravagant dimensions of Christ's love. Reach out and experience the breadth! Test its length! Plumb the depths! Rise to the heights! Live full lives, full in the fullness of God.

EPHESIANS 3:16-19 MSG

God bless you! May you receive the inner strength you need to succeed today. May the Holy Spirit empower you to not just get through your day but to have a fulfilling and exceptional day. May the talents that our God has graced you with flow out of you today with ease and grace.

We're still in the book of Ephesians, perusing Paul's letter to the church of Ephesus. The Message Bible Translation in Ephesians 3:7, dictated by Paul, says, "This is my life's work: helping people understand and respond to this Message." I love this translation of Paul's realization of his purpose. Although the Apostle Paul was in prison, he still desired to fulfill the "work" God called him to do. He goes on to say, "It came as a sheer gift to me, a real surprise, God handling all of the details."

I hope you have opened up your hearts to know God has given you as a gift to be used for His Glory. Also, it doesn't matter what state you're in or your current situation; God has a perfectly planned-out purpose for your existence. He loves you so much, and He wants you to be fulfilled. As I've stated many times, true peace and fulfillment only come from knowing Him, loving Him, and receiving and accepting His well-crafted intentions for your life.

In verses 14 and 15, Paul says, "…I get down on my knees before the Father Who is the Creator of everything in heaven and on earth." He goes on to say, "I pray that from His Glorious unlimited resources He will empower you with inner strength through His Spirit" (The Message and New Living Translation). Inner Strength from God's Holy Spirit is what we need every day to succeed. To be fulfilled every day, no matter what comes our way, we must have this Inner Strength.

As you open up your life to Him, allow the Holy Spirit to fill you and fulfill you with His Strength. It's so much better than yours. It starts with the tremendous power of His Love. The Love of God fills you with the strength to endure the hardest of issues and problems. When you experience this Love, you can't live without it, nor should you! God, your Father, desires you to be Encapsulated and Insulated with the Power of His Love.

While living this life, there are times we may believe the only way God can show us His Love is if every single thing works out perfectly. Paul was in the deepest, darkest, and most dank recesses of the worst kinds of imprisonment. Yet, he still wanted believers in Christ to experience this Love which gives Inner Strength to fulfill their purpose.

Perfect circumstances are not the accurate measure of God's Perfect Love. God wants to be right there with you in the trenches through the trials, tests, and tribulations in your life. It's how we show off God's Greatness to a dying world around us. This life we live on earth is not our final destination. So, while we're here, we can receive the Inner Strength not just to make it through, but with both feet planted firmly in God's Love, rise above, and live fulfilling lives.

My Notes

THIRTEEN

Drenched in God's Mercy

But you are God's chosen treasure —priests who are kings, a spiritual "nation" set apart as God's devoted ones. He called you out of darkness to experience his marvelous light, and now he claims you as his very own. He did this so that you would broadcast his glorious wonders throughout the world. For at one time you were not God's people, but now you are. At one time you knew nothing of God's mercy, because you hadn't received it yet, but now you are drenched with it!

1 Peter 2:9-10 TPT

God bless you today! You are God's Chosen Treasure, Hand Crafted by the Master Creator. You are born heir to the Kingdom of God and all that pertains to it. As soon as you said "yes" to Jesus, He presented to you the very best for your ultimate success. Everything you could possibly need is at your disposal. Whatever this day brings to you, you have the capability to handle it because you are in the Hand of Almighty God.

Jesus Christ gave His Life for us, and we are His. We are covered by His Love for us. We have been Hand Selected by Him for His Glorious Cause! According to God's Word in Matthew 16:18 in the Message Bible, you and I are a part of an expansive flourishing church that the kingdom of darkness cannot overthrow.

It goes on to say in verse 19: "And that's not all. You will have complete and free access to God's kingdom, keys to open any and every door: no more barriers between heaven and earth, earth and heaven. A yes on earth is yes in heaven. A no on earth is no in heaven."

You have authority here on earth because you have been given authority in Heaven. We need to acknowledge and recognize who we are; that's half of the battle that we face. You are a set apart devoted one, meaning your Heavenly Father is completely devoted to you.

As you continue to devote your heart to God, you have total access to God's Kingdom, freely going in and out as you please. You have the keys to open any and every door. You have the code to open up Heaven over your life. That's completely mind-boggling when you think about it. We can hardly believe we have that type of favor with God.

Our God is high above this world's tragedies, catastrophes, and difficulties. No matter what we face, we can face it with grace because we have been made priests, kings, and queens set apart as holy for our God. You may have heard the phrase, "get your head out of the clouds," but we should focus on the good things, the high things where our Heavenly Father is. He's the One we must allow to capture our attention.

It's easy to forget who you are and why you're here when you get caught up in what's going on all around you. The distractions in life are real; they are present and sometimes potent. Yet, even in this, we can rise above it. You, my dear one, can rise above it. It may not seem easy; it may be challenging, but you are a set-apart holy priest unto our God. He has called you out of darkness to experience His Marvelous Light.

You have received God's Mercy to sustain and support you through every dilemma and disappointment. At one time, you and I knew absolutely nothing of God's Mercy for our lives because we hadn't received it; we hadn't received Him. But now we are drenched in His Loving Mercy that carries us through so that we can be a living witness of His Amazing Grace.

This is what Peace in His Presence is all about.

My Notes

FOURTEEN

Our Ever-Present God

I will give thanks and praise to You, for I am fearfully and wonderfully made; Wonderful are Your works, And my soul knows it very well.

How precious also are Your thoughts to me, O God! How vast is the sum of them!

If I could count them, they would outnumber the sand. When I awake, I am still with You.

Psalm 139:14, 17-18 AMP

May the Lord of Heaven's Army reign and rule in your heart and mind today! I pray that you would take the time to magnify the Lord and allow Him to rise up big in you today. There is no God like our God Who rules the Heavens and will have the final say in the earth. He's a Great God, and when you lift Him up with praise and thanksgiving, He will lift you up to handle any and all worries, problems, and concerns. He's just that Good.

Psalm 139 in the Amplified Version is entitled "God's Omnipresence and Omniscience." This means that God is everywhere, and He knows everything. He's also Omnipotent, which declares He has All Power. This Psalm, written by David, speaks of our Lord, Who is the Self-Existing One. He is God Eternal Who formed and fashioned us and knows every single intricate detail of our beings. He has a perfect knowledge of us, and all of our thoughts and actions are open before Him.

The fact of your God's intimate personal knowledge of you shouldn't cause you to shy away from Him. Instead, you can run to Him, unashamed and unafraid, recognizing He Knows everything about you anyway. That is what David prayed in verse 1, "Lord You have searched me thoroughly and You have known me." When David ends Psalm 139 in verses 23 and 24, he cried out, "Search me thoroughly Oh God, and know my heart; Test me and know my anxious thoughts. And see if there is any wicked or hurtful way in me, and lead me in the everlasting way."

King David opens his heart and anxious thoughts to a God Who knows them anyway. There is so much peace when we open ourselves to God our Father. You can release every burden and cast down every care to the One Who cares so very much for you. Your God is interested in every detail of your life; nothing is too small or too great that He's not willing to handle. He's got the big and the small stuff. He wants to lead and guide you in the right way, the way to everlasting life.

You are so precious to God that He took such great care in creating you. David expresses in verse 3 that your God is intimately acquainted with all your ways. Verse 14 says that you are fearfully and wonderfully made. What does that mean exactly? You have been reverently and marvelously distinguished to be fabulous! Oh yes you have! You are admirable! You are incredible! You are amazing! Don't take my word for it. That is exactly what your God says about you! When you see yourself in the mirror, I hope these words are what you say about yourself.

David knew this is true, declaring "wonderful are Your works and my soul knows it very well." You may not see yourself as having all of these fantastic attributes, but you most certainly do! Why? Because your God says it is so. Every thought God has of you is precious, beautiful, and extravagant in number and His thoughts of you last all the day long.

I hope you know how marvelous you are! Today and every day, when you wake up, remember your Amazing God, Who is waiting for you to arise, wants you to realize you are positively wonderful! He looks at you with all-consuming love in His eyes; you are that precious to Him.

My Notes

FIFTEEN

The Lord Rescues Me

"I love You [fervently and devotedly], O Lord, my strength." The Lord is my rock, my fortress, and the One who rescues me; My God, my rock and strength in whom I trust and take refuge; My shield, and the horn of my salvation, my high tower—my stronghold. I call upon the Lord, who is worthy to be praised; And I am saved from my enemies...

The Lord lives, blessed be my rock; And may the God of my salvation be exalted....

Psalm 18:1-3, 46 AMP

Bless the Mighty Name of the Lord today! May you find true Peace in His Presence as you take this moment to Pause in His Presence. When you take just a few minutes to sit down before Him, take a deep breath and invite Him into your space, He'll be right there. He's just waiting for you to pause.

David wrote this Psalm as a praise break when the Lord rescued him from his enemy King Saul, who grew jealous of David because the people seemed to celebrate David more than Saul. God's Favor on David's life caused King Saul to become his enemy.

When the women came out to welcome the men home from battle in 1 Samuel 18:7, they sang, "Saul has slain his thousands and David his ten thousands," which, of course, angered the king. Because of the king's jealousy toward David, an evil spirit was released upon him, and he literally sought to kill David at every turn. It's devastating what jealousy and hatred can do to a person's psyche!

Although David was hated by King Saul with a visceral hatred, David always sought to appease his king. David was anointed to worship the Lord with singing, writing music, and playing the harp or the lyre. His musical therapy brought solace and peace to King Saul, so he wouldn't be tormented.

Music therapy can be used for our well-being right now. Listening and playing the right kind of music helps to calm the savage beast within. You may not be tormented by an evil spirit, but you may be dealing with some complex issues, and you need God's Peace and Presence to carry you through.

Every day is a great day to worship and give glory to our God. Lifting your devoted worship to God matters in the best and worst of times. David always took time to worship and praise his God. So, when he became king, praise and worship were one of the first things he established as a priority.

David writes in Psalm 68:1, "Let God arise, let his enemies be scattered." As he continues to bless the Lord throughout this Psalm, a combination of the King James version and The New Living translation in verse 25 says, "The singers went before, the players on instruments followed after; between them are young women playing tambourines." He then encouraged the rest of Israel, which he called the congregation, to join in and bless the Lord. Praising and worshiping God was vital; it was necessary for their victory in every battle.

I absolutely love how the first verse of Psalm 18 starts by declaring, "I love You [fervently and devotedly], O Lord, my strength." What an extraordinary admission! What a heartfelt devotion to God. Good music can bring you to a place of solace and peace in victories, battles, high times, and the low times. But, most importantly, you can lift a praise of thanksgiving towards your God out of your own mouth. He's ready to hear and receive it, empowering you in all situations.

My Notes

SIXTEEN

God is Our Light in the Darkness

This is the message [of God's promised revelation] which we have heard from Him and now announce to you, that God is Light [He is holy, His message is truthful, He is perfect in righteousness], and in Him there is no darkness at all [no sin, no wickedness, no imperfection].

1 John 1:5 AMP

Blessings to you today. May you be filled with the Joy of the Lord. Our joy isn't predicated on our emotions, inner turmoil, or exterior circumstances. Instead, we can call on the Joy of the Lord to be our strength even in the worst of times.

God desires each one of us to know that He is Light in the darkness. When we can't see which way to turn or what direction to go, He'll be right there to give us answers of peace. But, sometimes, to receive this message of peace, we must be quiet in order to recognize His Voice.

He is Perfect in all of His Ways and His Direction for your life is perfectly formed just for you. Allow Him to illuminate the dark places in you; allow His Light to shine on the darkest deepest parts of your psyche. Your God wants you to have victory in all areas of your life, not just the things seen by others.

It doesn't matter how dark, dismal, or dirty those areas may be; your Heavenly Father, your Holy God, desires to be right there healing and helping. Even if these offenses in us continue to rise, the Holy Spirit will be present as a Help to bring complete deliverance to every issue. We just have to let Him into our darkness.

Yes, we live in the Light of a Perfect God; only Truth lives in Him. He will only give us the Truth. The enemy of our soul is the one who continues to perpetuate lies. We overcome the lies with God's Truth. The Word of the Lord tells us we are the redeemed of the Lord; we are the called out ones (Psalm 107:2; 1 Peter 2:9). We are the head and not the tail; we are above only and not beneath (Deuteronomy 28:13). These Truths in God's

Word are for all who say "yes" to Jesus.

This Perfect God loves and cherishes imperfect people: you and me. His Perfect Love covers our imperfect lives.

We have Perfect Promises to receive from Him just because He loves us. Regardless of how we feel, what we experience, or our past issues, God's Word overtakes every lie of the wicked. It covers every negative trial and causes us to triumph even through tragedy. Always be open to God's Light and His Love; it will dispel your darkness.

My Notes

SEVENTEEN

The Great Shepherd Makes You Great!

Now may the God of peace who brought up our Lord Jesus from the dead, that great Shepherd of the sheep, through the blood of the everlasting covenant, make you complete in every good work to do His will, working in you what is well pleasing in His sight, through Jesus Christ, to whom be glory forever and ever. Amen.

HEBREWS 13:20-21 NKJV

Hi! I pray the Abundance of God's Favor rests upon you and your entire household today. May you be Abundantly Provided for in Christ Jesus. May you experience the Manifold Wisdom of God as you maneuver throughout this day. May God speak to your heart and bring rest to your mind as the decisions that need to be made today unfold. May His Peace be yours today.

I shared Hebrews 13:20-21 from the Amplified Classic Version in my first devotional, *Pause In His Presence*. This time I would like to share these same verses from the New King James Version, entitled "Benediction, Final Exhortation, Farewell."

Now theologians are not exactly sure who wrote Hebrews, seeing that there is no formal greeting to begin the letter. Yet, if we look at the order the books were put together in the New Testament portion of the Bible, we see Hebrews as the last book that could have been written or dictated by the Apostle Paul. The following books are in succession: James, First and Second Peter, First, Second and Third John, Jude, and Revelations.

I pondered what was on the author's mind if these written words were their last. I find it intriguing that these last verses of Scripture in Hebrews are entitled with such finality. It gives the context of the weight of these words much more meaning. These weren't words begging for some last-minute help to be released from their predicament if they were indeed in a negative situation.

A compelling argument is given throughout the pages of Hebrews, encouraging us that Jesus is so much Better than anything we can possibly imagine. He's Better than the angels. He's Better than Moses. He's so much Better than the Law. He's Better than any blood sacrifice. He's the Ultimate Blood Sacrifice, and He is so much Better than anything else we think we may need.

After sharing all of this, the writer encourages in chapter 13, verses 20-21: "May the God of Peace... make you complete...." According to the Amplified Bible Classic, that means He will strengthen, complete, perfect, and make you what you ought to be and equip you with everything good.

Oh, this is so amazing! He wants you to understand that you are made complete in Him to do His Will. Allowing Him to continually work with you, in you, and even for you is where His Peace steps in to complete you so that while you live this life, you will have no lack. This is Good News! You, my dear, are equipped to do the work! The God of the Universe, this Holy and Great God, has you in His sights. He's with you on your journey every day.

This letter was written to the newly converted Jewish Christians and placed in this Holy Book for our benefit. Whatever the fate may have been for the author of the book of Hebrews, they pushed to the end doing the Work and the Will of God. This dedicated servant of the Lord wanted you and me to know God, a Consuming Fire (Hebrews 12:29), Who is the Author and Giver of our peace (Hebrews 13:20 AMPC).

He's with us, in us, and desires to work through us for His Purpose and His Glory! Whatever God calls you to do, He equips you to do it. You're not in this by yourself. It's in you to be great!

My Notes

EIGHTEEN

Lift Up Praises to Our God

Hallelujah! Praise the Lord! Go ahead, praise the Lord, all you loving servants of God! Keep it up! Praise him some more! For the glorious name of the Lord is blessed forever and ever. From sunrise-brilliance to sunset-beauty, lift up his praise from dawn to dusk! For he rules on high over the nations with a glory that outshines even the heavens.

Psalm 113:1-4 TPT

Hey there! It's time to take a praise break and glorify your God! You may not have a specific reason at this moment to give God Glory! Yet, you can go ahead and praise Him anyway! We are the loving servants of the Lord, and because we do indeed love Him, we should praise Him. Anytime!

Even our Lord and Savior Jesus Christ lifted a song to God before being crucified on the cross (Matthew 26:30; Mark 14:26). While having His Last Supper with His Disciples, He led them in a worship song to the Heavenly Father. We should always take the time to lift up praise and worship to our Holy God. When we're heavy, we can praise Him. When we're happy, we can praise Him. When facing a challenging or even horrific situation, like our Savior prepared to experience, we can still lift praises to God.

No one knows who wrote Psalm 113. Some Bible scholars believe this Psalm was written by Moses. Still others believe David wrote it. Nonetheless, one thing is noted, this Psalm, like many others, was sung during the time of the Passover. So now, Christian believers sing this Psalm, celebrating what our Lord and Savior accomplished for us over 2,000 years ago. His Blood Sacrifice is so worth celebrating today. Jesus got up from the grave so that you and I could get up and get over every graphic situation that may have plagued our lives.

We have a reason to lift our hands and shout praises unto God! He is so Worthy of exuberant celebration, exhilarated praise, and our heartfelt expression of worship. He made the difficult choice to be hung on a cross until He breathed His last breath for every soul on the planet. Because of His Ultimate

Sacrifice, we have the privilege to live eternally in Heaven with Him! Earth is not our last stop.

We have an eternity in Heaven to look forward to, and the way to get there is through the Blood of Jesus Christ. He's our Goal and our Prize, and nothing matters without Him! His Blood heals and makes us whole. His Blood delivers and sets us free. We can be free from this world's delusional desires for earthly conquests. It's not to say we aren't able to have the things in this world; however, we cannot allow the things in this world to have us.

We are engrafted into His Beautiful Family when we receive and accept Him. We are His. There's safety and reassurance when we realize we're under the Protection of our Sovereign Savior. Life is worth living when we're living this life with Him. We have a reason to open our eyes in the morning, knowing our God has given us another day to live joyfully in His Presence.

Giving Him all of the Glory due to Him and allowing His Goodness to rest over our lives is why we are here on planet earth. Furthermore, we are here to show the world the blessedness of living a life that glorifies our Heavenly Father. So go ahead and Praise the Lord. Then, Praise Him some more. He Alone is Worthy!

My Notes

NINETEEN

Finding Joy in Hard Times

Don't run from tests and hardships, brothers and sisters. As difficult as they are, you will ultimately find joy in them; if you embrace them, your faith will blossom under pressure and teach you true patience as you endure. And true patience brought on by endurance will equip you to complete the long journey and cross the finish line—mature, complete, and wanting nothing.

JAMES 1:2-4 THE VOICE

Hi! God bless you for opening up your devotion today. Every time you open up and read the Word of God, it's an opportunity to receive your victory. Yes, by being a partaker in God's Word, the enemy becomes defeated in all areas of your life.

I pray the Word helps you navigate through your day today. His Word is designed not just to be a balm to heal your soul; it's a tool to guide you through life's tests, trials, and even tumultuous seasons. I pray you're strengthened by the Scripture reading for today.

I don't know about you, but I am not encouraged when I go through hard times. I am not excited when I see a test coming my way, and I don't get happy when trials hit my house. I don't like it one bit. I have to speak the Word of God and tell myself to "count it all joy" when negative stuff happens. The bad stuff isn't joyful, but we can count it and mix it with joy so that we can go through our test with God's Grace and Peace.

We can find and experience Joy when hardships hit our house! James, the brother of Jesus, encourages us not to turn away and run from hardships, tests, and trials. But instead, we should understand this: "As difficult as they are, we will ultimately find joy in them."

The Scriptures are given to us so we can respond using the Word as our Governor and Guide. Therefore, with the Word as our constant companion, we can stand in the face of difficulties and walk through tests and trials victorious no matter the outcome. James said, as soon as we embrace the difficult times we experience, the sooner we will find joy in them, and our faith will blossom and grow.

Can you imagine facing your tough trials with joy? That seems the opposite of how we usually react when trouble hits our lives. The first thing we experience is undoubtedly not joy because it takes a focused effort to embrace challenging moments in life and then choose to face them with joy. That's just it: we have to make an effort to focus on how Great our God is right in the middle of the test and trial.

It's easy to look around at the problems and pressures against us. We tend to focus on everything right before us, especially when a major issue hits us hard. We do not see that our God is right there with us. The true measure of our faith is not when everything is going well but when everything isn't. When trouble comes, our faith is under fire, and we still need to have a focused faith in our Father through it all.

There will be times when we don't understand everything that is happening in our lives or happening around us. When struggles come to shake us and throw us off course, that's when we must lock into our hope and trust in God. We have to understand that the test is not meant to break us, but instead allow it to make us able to endure all things.

Endurance brings about true patience through tribulation, and that's how our faith is made strong. We endure to the end, exercising our patience. Unless pressure is applied, faith isn't strengthened. A bodybuilder can't build muscle strength unless there's extra weight placed on the bar. They call it strength resistance.

Without pressure, the essence of who you're meant to be is not recognized. If you've ever cooked with a pressure cooker, you understand that pressure and heat cause the food to turn out delicious. If you release the pressure too soon, all those blended flavors and seasonings won't combine to make that perfect meal. I know we don't want to go through a pressurized cooking experience or a fiery situation, but the Word of God says you will go through the fire and not be burned (Isaiah 43:2). The pressures of life won't take you out.

When you go through the terrible things in life, you've got to call on the Joy of the Lord to be your strength (Nehemiah 8:10; Psalm 21:1). Call on Joy, and then you count it all joy. Let Joy strengthen you to endure until the end of the trauma. As you embrace Joy, you will find you are becoming more mature, completely satisfied in your God, not wanting or lacking in the good things you need to succeed!

My Notes

TWENTY

Wisdom for Your Journey

If you don't have all the wisdom needed for this journey, then all you have to do is ask God for it; and God will grant all that you need. He gives lavishly and never scolds you for asking.

The key is that your request be anchored by your single-minded commitment to God. Those who depend only on their own judgment are like those lost on the seas, carried away by any wave or picked up by any wind.

JAMES 1:5-6 THE VOICE

May our Lord Keep you and Comfort you today as you continue to embrace His Instructions for your life. May you experience His Peace in your heart and mind as you take a moment to Pause in His Presence.

We continue in this passage found in the letter James wrote to the Jewish Christians scattered all over the world during the first century. After he exhorts us in verses 2 through 4 to embrace hard times with joy, he instructs us to receive wisdom for our journey. We need the Wisdom of God for our everyday life experiences. We need Wisdom for the hard times we face and the hard decisions we have to make.

Receiving God's Wisdom starts by seeking Him in His Word. We have to make His Word our priority each day. By applying His Word daily with His Guidance and Love, we have access to Godly Wisdom working in our lives. That's not the final step, but it's an important one. Allowing the Word of God to work in your life makes your heart pliable to hear God's Voice of Wisdom.

He'll give you instructions in wisdom in the midst of your plight when you take the time to listen. He leads and guides you to the person who will speak words of wise counsel to help with your decision-making process. He also speaks to you about the place to find the answers to wisdom.

We cannot decide to devise our own plan, or as James in this translation says, depend only on our judgment and ask for Wisdom from God. In this, we become double-minded, going back and forth in our heads, confused, and not receiving anything. Either trust God's Wisdom or your own way; it can't be both.

After his father King David passed away, King Solomon asked God for wisdom for the task of leading God's people. According to 1 Kings 3:9, he asked for an understanding heart. God was so pleased with his request that he gave him wisdom, understanding, and resources for success.

In the Hebrew translation, Solomon's request for understanding implies hearing intelligently with attention and obedience. This means that with great intent, we obey what God's Word says concerning the wisdom for our lives. If we adhere to His Word in the little things, we'll be more likely to obey His Word in the big things. This takes, as James describes, "a single-minded commitment to God."

James 1:5 correlates with 1 Kings 3:9, letting us know that asking God for wisdom is the very thing that separates us from failing in life and having a fulfilling life. Examining the Scriptures shows us that it pleases God when we ask Him for His Wisdom. Reading the Proverbs, called the Book of Wisdom, is an excellent source of wisdom daily. There are 31 Proverbs, one for each day of the month.

Wisdom from the Lord can come through seeking God and godly counsel. Sometimes the wise counsel we receive is not what we want to hear, but it is what we need.

Don't reject wisdom when it comes to you. Instead, receive it with thanksgiving and seek how to apply it to your life's journey.

In this, you won't be tossed around, carried away by the waves and the winds of life. Instead, you can be anchored in the Word and walk in wisdom.

My Notes

TWENTY-ONE

Relief With The Lord

Come to Me, all you who labor and are heavy-laden and overburdened, and I will cause you to rest. [I will ease and relieve and refresh your souls.]

Take My yoke upon you and learn of Me, for I am gentle (meek) and humble (lowly) in heart, and you will find rest (relief and ease and refreshment and recreation and blessed quiet) for your souls.

MATTHEW 11:28-29 AMPC

Vacations are lovely, and I certainly recommend them. Setting aside time to relax is beneficial. Doing fun outdoor activities is incredibly refreshing. Yet real rest, complete rest, rest that heals your mind, body, and soul comes from resting in the Presence of the Lord. There's absolutely no rest that's better. May our Heavenly Father cause you to find the rest you need that only comes from the His Presence. You won't experience true holistic Peace without God's Holy Presence.

The Presence of the Lord is where you find Peace. Jesus takes the time to call all who labor in any capacity and are heavy, overburdened, overwhelmed, and just plain tired. He says, "I Will cause you to rest." According to the Amplified Bible, He says that He "will ease and relieve and refresh our souls" when we take the time to come to Him.

Our souls consist of our feelings, thoughts, and emotions and are a very real and natural part of us. It is the essence of our reasoning. It is the seat or primary place where our decision-making is conducted. It distinguishes our likes from our dislikes.

Our personality is mainly produced out of our souls. It is the core essence of who we are before we became born again. We react and interact from this place, especially when our spirit man is not renewed continuously by the Word of God. Our souls can sometimes have full control.

Jesus takes out the time to speak to us about our souls. He desires to minister to our souls. He takes the time to care about our souls, bringing help, healing, answers, and relief. He explains to us very plainly through the Scriptures that to receive this rest, this ease, this relief, and this refreshing happens when we bind ourselves to Him.

To take His Yoke is to permanently couple, connect, and tie ourselves to Him. It's the example of two farm animals tied together, placing a beam on them so they can work the fields in unison together. Both animals doing the same work, carrying the same burden together. This way, if one is stronger, the burden becomes lighter on the weaker animal.

The Call of God on your life is His Yoke and only accomplished with His Leading and not your own. Jesus says, "I want you to stop carrying your own burden and carry mine instead." His Yoke is light and easy. His burden won't cause you to buckle under pressure or give out before completing the task. Taking the time to learn of the Lord means spending time with Him in His Word. This occurs through reading devotions like this one, hearing the preached Word of God through church attendance, and praying with the Scriptures.

Instead of being consumed with our issues, problems, worries, and concerns, we should be consumed with the Lord and all His Amazing Promises. When we come to Him willingly and freely, He gives us His rest. Likewise, we find rest when we commit ourselves and connect with Him without limitation, experiencing rest for our souls and our everyday decision-making. That's double rest and ultimate peace.

My Notes

TWENTY-TWO

You are a Work of Art

"For we are His workmanship [His own master work, a work of art], created in Christ Jesus [reborn from above—spiritually transformed, renewed, ready to be used] for good works, which God prepared [for us] beforehand [taking paths which He set], so that we would walk in them [living the good life which He prearranged and made ready for us]."

EPHESIANS 2:10 AMP

Hi, God bless you today. I pray that you are doing well and not just okay. My prayer for you this day is that you would indeed be well—mind, body, and soul. I pray His Peace surrounds you in such a way that regardless of what you have to face today, you would be governed, guided, and graced with the Peace of God.

Ephesians 2:10 in the Amplified Bible says, "we are His workmanship, [His own master work, a work of art]...." We have been handcrafted by the Creator. You, my dear, are a perfect work of God-art. You are an accomplishment by the Master Crafter, pure, organic, and complete in every way. When we suffer from guilt, shame and insecurities, these thoughts and feelings are not from God above but from the depths of hell below. They are demonic warfare at its greatest attack.

The devil, who is the deceiver, wants you to feel less than, lowering yourself, looking down on yourself, and never looking up to your God. However, that is never God's desire for you; He always wants you to recognize who you are. When you discover who you are, who you really are, you can see the possibilities of what God has for your future. You can get up and look up from any disappointment, distraction, and discouraging thing that comes up against you. You can fulfill your God-Ordained Purpose in this life with the Power and Backing of God Almighty Himself!

When you receive Jesus Christ as your personal Lord and Savior, you have been reborn from above —spiritually transformed, renewed, and ready to be used for good works. Good works are the God-Works your God has predesignated for you to accomplish by His Will and Grace. You've got some good work to do on this side of Heaven. According to the Message Translation, this work is something we better get busy doing.

We have been placed on this planet to work. Not just to work a nine to five, get off, go home and go to sleep. You have a good work, a great work which is a God-Work that He has divinely designed and explicitly pre-portioned just for you to do. We all have work to do! When we all get in there and do what God has handcrafted us to do, we can accomplish so much for the Kingdom of God. Just by doing your part, the Kingdom of God is moved a few more steps forward.

You've been graced and gifted for this work in the Kingdom. When God made you, He knew exactly what He was doing and didn't make any mistakes. You are what you are by the Grace of God (1 Corinthians 15:10). His Grace is all you need to fulfill His Will for your beautifully designed life. This life is the good life our God prearranged for you. So, I hope that you live it to the fullest. In this, you will be completely fulfilled!

My Notes

TWENTY-THREE

Get Wisdom

My child, never forget the things I have taught you.
Store my commands in your heart.
If you do this, you will live many years,
and your life will be satisfying.

PROVERBS 3:1-2 NLT

Proverbs is known as the book of Wisdom. Most of the compositions in this book were inspired by Solomon, who received words of wisdom from his father, David. The Hebrew translation of a proverb defines it as "sentences or poems of ethical wisdom." David's "sayings" or words of wisdom to his son Solomon were written for our benefit even today.

It's a great practice to write down the precious words of wisdom you receive over your lifetime.

As we follow Solomon's life, we see areas where he didn't always remember to apply the wise counsel that his father shared. Occasionally, he allowed what was going on around him to throw him off course. His thoughts are also written in Ecclesiastes to help us see some of his dilemmas.

Although we read about areas of struggle in Solomon's and David's lives, we can still pick up many beautiful nuggets of wisdom from these great writings. Nobody is perfect, not a single one of us. That is why we constantly need wise and godly counsel.

We also need to humble ourselves to be able to receive from those who walk in wisdom. Despite the mistakes we make and the missteps we take, receiving godly wisdom to live this life is vital.

Solomon writes what his father shared with him: *If you don't forget the things I've taught you and keep them in your heart, you will live a long, satisfying life* (Proverbs 3:1). Wow, that's a significant promise for all of us. When we listen and adhere to wise counsel, things go well! But, of course, we don't always get the wise counsel we need. Either we don't realize we need it, we don't recognize it's available for us to receive it, or we may be too afraid or proud to ask for it.

Yet in Proverbs 3, we see that wisdom through wise counsel must be a staple in our decision-making process. When we don't make good decisions, it can have adverse effects. I know I've made mistakes in my decisions and have gone down paths I shouldn't have taken. But the beautiful thing about life is it's never too late to make a midterm correction and change direction! Aren't you grateful for that fact? I certainly am!

Over the years, we've been taught that our daily reading should include at least a Proverb a day and perhaps five Psalms in the evening. There are 31 Proverbs and a 150 Psalms in our Bible. There's a whole lot to devour on any given day. Our hearts should always be open to the wisdom we need for everyday living.

Never close your heart and mind to wisdom. We don't know as much as we think. Proverbs 4:7 in the Amplified Bible Classic says, "The beginning of wisdom is: get Wisdom (skillful and godly wisdom)!" Thus, we must go after it! We should "get wisdom" because it is the "principal thing." It is the essential most primary thing we need to operate in this life that we have the privilege of living. The Amplified Version of this verse says wisdom is "preeminent!"

Wisdom needs to be pretty high on our list of priorities of the things we need to obtain. Whatever else you try to get in this life, put godly wisdom on the top of your to-do list. It will cost you, sometimes your pride, your personality, and even people, but it's worth the price. Listen to wisdom, receive wise counsel, seek it out, and then apply it to your life. Then, proceed to live this good life that God has just for you!

My Notes

TWENTY-FOUR

Loyalty and Kindness Deep-Rooted in Our Hearts

Never let loyalty and kindness leave you!
Tie them around your neck as a reminder.
Write them deep within your heart.
Then you will find favor with both God and people,
and you will earn a good reputation.

PROVERBS 3:3-4 NLT

Today we're continuing with our devotion in Proverbs chapter three. My prayer for you today is as you take the time to read and soak in the Word of the Lord, His Word will fill your heart to do His Will. When we make His Word our priority, we are taking the time to make an effort to live out this life of love and liberty with our Lord. I pray you witness the results of this blessed life our God has for you to live.

In the Amplified Bible, Proverbs chapter three says, "Do not let mercy and kindness and truth leave you [instead let these qualities define you]...." This means we must allow a certain quality of character to shape who we are at the fundamental level. Oh my goodness! That takes a lot of effort to accomplish, especially for those who may not exhibit these attributes naturally. Even the best of us can lose our cool once in a while, so the Scripture encourages us never to let these things leave us.

Being loyal and kind is easy when those around us treat us right. You don't have to tell me to be nice to nice people. I can be loyal to loyal people, and it's simple to be kind to genuinely kind people. However, when folks aren't so great, we must remember to stay calm and be kind. That's exactly what the author is encouraging the readers of this proverb to do. He says to take loyalty and kindness and tie them around your neck.

Anytime you have something tied around your neck, you'll remember that it's there. So before you can react irrationally to a situation, loyalty and kindness can constantly remind you, "Hey! I'm right here wrapped around your neck." The verse doesn't stop there; it goes on to say to write them deep within your heart. We do this so we never forget before we do or say anything. Loyalty and kindness are the rudimentary fundamentals of our hearts. These traits are to be sown deep inside of us. Simply stated, even when we're not feeling it, we cannot help but be merciful to others, showing kindness and love. I've heard it said that "if our Christianity does not make us kind, it is not real."

This verse also comes with an amazing promise. We will find favor with God and people and acquire a good reputation! Favor with God is the ultimate gift we can receive. He makes rough patches smooth for us and can make crooked things straight (Isaiah 40:4). God can turn things around in our favor because we have favor with Him. And we can be encouraged to know we've done everything in our power to respond in truth and love.

Though conditions may not be as favorable as we'd like, we can still allow the attributes of mercy, loyalty, and kindness to be in our hearts and the cornerstone of our actions. A reputation for responding well under fire will keep favor coming your way.

Proverbs 3:1 in the New King James Bible says, "My son, do not forget my law, But let your heart keep my commandments." The wisdom of a wise father or mother figure passed down to sons and daughters is priceless. When we follow those who walk in wisdom, we benefit from their knowledge for our betterment.

Our Heavenly Father desires to enhance our lives with His Wisdom. Verse two says, "For length of days and long life and peace" are promised when we apply words of wise counsel.

I wanted us to grab hold of each verse's depth of meaning. Walking in wisdom and understanding will lead us in our actions of loyalty and kindness. They go hand in hand.

I want to have God's Hand of Favor over my life! I'm sure you do as well! We need the favor of God. So, if favor is connected to following wise counsel and responding to negative stuff with mercy, then I'm all in. And I hope you're all in this thing as well! Receive favor with God and people and gain a good reputation in the process!

My Notes

TWENTY-FIVE

Complete Trust in The Lord

Trust in the Lord completely, and do not rely on your own opinions. With all your heart, rely on him to guide you, and he will lead you in every decision you make. Become intimate with him in whatever you do, and he will lead you wherever you go.

Proverbs 3:5-6 TPT

As we continue with these first few stanzas found in Proverbs, let's delve into verses five and six. The Word of God holds so much power and promise when we meditate on its meaning for our lives. I pray the added attention to God's Word continues to penetrate your heart when you reread them today.

I love how verse five starts with"Trust in the Lord completely!" The word completely is interchanged with "Trust in the Lord with all thine heart" in the King James Bible. Completely means wholly, totally, ultimately, and unconditionally. When broken down further, it means without limitations, without questions; thoroughly from the beginning to the end. It's worth taking the time to fully understand, comprehend, and take in.

Trusting God and not in our limited knowledge and opinions is a safe and secure place for you and me to rest. We serve a God Who is Gracious, Loving, and Kind. He does not hold grudges, nor does He make mistakes. He has us in the palm of His Hands (Isaiah 49:16). There is absolutely no other place or person that is more solid than our God. In Psalm 27:10-11, David said, "Though my father and mother forsake me, you will take care of me, teach me your ways, and show me what to do."

We serve a God we can trust to lead, teach, and direct us if we follow Him. Throughout Scripture, the Lord's ultimate goal is to get His children to trust Him without reservation and concern. Can you imagine giving God complete control to the point that you rely on Him with every decision you make?

It's imperative for each of us who names the Name of Jesus Christ to get to know Him intimately. We must invite Him into every aspect of our lives, not shutting Him out of situations we think we have handled or problems we may be ashamed of. He knows it all anyway. So, we might as well let Him in there.

Listen for His Voice, look for His Leading, learn from the teachings of Godly instructors and allow His Word to live fully in your life. This is how we become intimate with the One we say we love with our whole heart. This is how we live our blessed life!

My Notes

TWENTY-SIX

Kiss the Son

Serve and worship the awe-inspiring God. Recognize his greatness and bow before him, trembling with reverence in his presence. Fall face down before him and kiss the Son before his anger is roused against you. Remember that his wrath can be quickly kindled! But many blessings are waiting for all who turn aside to hide themselves in him!

PSALM 2:11-12 TPT

Blessing to you today! May you receive God's Wonderful Grace and Mercy for your day. May you be infused with His Love and Strength to be empowered for whatever the day may bring.

This Psalm, not attributed to any known author, is classified as a Messianic song because it references the Son of God. We as believers in Jesus Christ have this mandate: To worship our Lord and Savior continually. The authority in the script suggests that this is a commandment and not an invitation.

The directness of the tone is not necessarily speaking to God's People per se. The Psalmist aims to reach those who aren't serving and worshiping the Only True and Living God. Yet still, as God's chosen people, we need a reminder every now and then to bend our knees and bow our heads before our Gracious God. He is Holy and oh so Worthy of our reverence.

We should take time each day and throughout our day to Honor and give Glory to our God. Just take a moment, if you can right where you are, to take in a deep breath. As you breathe in and out, begin to speak the Name of Jesus. I know you can sense His Calming Presence within you right now.

Worship expresses our heartfelt adoration for our Holy God. Honestly, when we take the time to lift our hands or even lift our hearts to God, something within us lifts. We experience peace and well-being right in the middle of everything around us going completely awry. Worship invites God into the mess with us, giving us the strength and boost we need to keep going.

My favorite part of this Psalm says to "kiss the Son." We can correctly interpret this phrase as speaking of Jesus, the Son of God. As soon as we read these words, they should inspire intimacy, closeness, affection, and love. That's precisely what God desires from us and what He desires to give to us: His Affection and His Love.

His Affection towards us and for each of us should affect us in ways that change our hearts and lives for good. His Love can heal the pain, sorrow, and afflictions of this world's hurt and harm. You don't have to stay the same, hurting and never healing. You can turn aside right now, kiss the Son, and hide in the shelter of His Care!

My Notes

TWENTY-SEVEN

God's Breath of Life is Found in His Word

God has transmitted his very substance into every Scripture, for it is God-breathed. It will empower you by its instruction and correction, giving you the strength to take the right direction and lead you deeper into the path of godliness. Then you will be God's servant, fully mature and perfectly prepared to fulfill any assignment God gives you.

2 Timothy 3:16-17 TPT

Hi, I sure hope you're doing well today! Once again, thank you for taking another moment to peruse this devotional. I pray you're blessed by what's shared today and that you'd also take the time to share it with others. We can pray for special encounters to speak with people around us about God's Word. Let's believe He'll open the hearts and minds of those who are willing to receive His Love.

We have the privilege to live this God-filled life with purpose on purpose. We were born to fulfill God's Perfect Will on this side of Heaven. So, every day we get to open our eyes is an opportunity to make an impact on our world. It doesn't matter how large or small we imagine that impact is; it's part of the whole package of God's Plan.

We've often heard God's Word is a Promise Book; well, it's also a Purpose Book. The Passion Translation of this passage of Scripture says, "God has transmitted His very substance into every Scripture, for it is God-breathed." These illuminating words right here should make a significant impact on our psyche!

Every time we pick up the Word of God and realize that Jehovah Himself is infused on every page, we can receive power from His Word to overcome every obstacle and to do His Will. That's "inner strength" straight from the throne room of God Almighty.

So, as you read God's Holy Script today, be empowered by the instructions and the corrections you receive. Allow His Word to mobilize you into action, "giving you the strength to take the right direction and lead you deeper into the path of godliness." We find real joy here, right in the center of His Will and right in the center of His Love for each one of us.

Doing what God has set you on planet earth to do is where development and devotion towards Him must take place. We can't do anything without Him, and we need Him for every step we take and every move we make.

You and I, child of God, have an assignment to fulfill before we go to Heaven to be with our Lord. Read the Word of God, expecting to experience more of Him. Not just knowing and reciting more Scriptures but knowing your Heavenly Father more intimately.

A true servant wants to get to know the one they serve so they can serve them better. To serve God better is to know Him more. Be empowered to seek the Father through His Word so you can know His Will and be truly fulfilled.

My Notes

TWENTY-EIGHT

Be Revived Again!

Revive us again, O God! I know you will! Give us a fresh start! Then all your people will taste your joy and gladness. Pour out even more of your love on us! Reveal more of your kindness and restore us back to you! Now I'll listen carefully for your voice and wait to hear whatever you say. Let me hear your promise of peace— the message every one of your godly lovers longs to hear. Don't let us in our ignorance turn back from following you.

PSALM 85:6-8 TPT

Hey, blessings to you! Let's take the time to rejoice in the Lord today! It's always good to take a moment right where you are to lift your hands and Glorify your God! I pray your day is amazing and filled with God moments of hearing His Voice in your ear.

Psalm 85 is known as a prophetic song written and sung by the sons of Korah. If you remember anything about Korah, he was the one who led a rebellion against Moses and Aaron that did not end well. This account is found in the book of Numbers.

What blesses me about the sons of Korah is that their ancestors pride and arrogance along with their father's sin did not cause their hearts to be hardened against the Lord. On the contrary, these descendants of Korah became great anointed psalmists who ministered to the Lord in the office of the priesthood.

Our family lineage does not have to determine our heritage, one way or the other. Whatever decisions made or actions taken by our ancestors don't have to affect our future. It doesn't have to make or break you. You must forge your own path, make good choices, and not blame the past for what takes place in your future.

These descendants decided to go after God for themselves. Calling out to Him in adoration and thanksgiving, they beckoned the Lord in this Psalm, saying, "Revive us again, Oh God." I love what they say next! "I know you will!" What a total confident expectation they had in the Lord their God! No matter what we do, where we go, or how far away we get, God will bring us back to Him and revive us again when we call out to Him.

When you know and understand the generational curses in your family, you can break the chains from your life and not allow them to plague you or corrupt your future. Unfortunately, some followed Korah's lead by rebelling against the Lord and His man Moses. These families suffered significant harm because of it. Every choice we make is important; who you choose to follow matters.

In this Psalm, the sons of Korah ask God for "a fresh start," stating, "Then all your people will taste your joy and gladness!" They asked God to pour out even more of His Love, His Kindness, and to be restored back to Him. These brothers knew their position with the Father and weren't ashamed or afraid to ask for it!

That's the boldness God desires from each one of us who call God our Father. Don't be scared to go to your Heavenly Father with boldness. Declare to Him that you desire to hear His Voice and follow His Instructions for your life. If you need more encouragement, read this Psalm in totality and receive every blessing our God has for you!

My Notes

TWENTY-NINE

Lift Up a Continual Praise to Our God

Let the whole earth sing to the Lord! Each day proclaim the good news that he saves. Publish his glorious deeds among the nations. Tell everyone about the amazing things he does. Great is the Lord! He is most worthy of praise! He is to be feared above all gods. The gods of other nations are mere idols, but the Lord made the heavens! Honor and majesty surround him; strength and joy fill his dwelling.

1 Chronicles 16:23-27 NLT

David secured the Ark of the Lord from the home of Obededom. Celebrations and shouts of praise and thanksgiving were heard from miles around, and that was just from David himself! This king tried and failed once before to bring the Ark back to Jerusalem with disastrous results. The Ark of the Covenant represented (during this time) the Presence and Power of the Lord (1 Chronicles 15:29).

This sacred encasement with two large angels placed on top with a seat in the middle called the Mercy Seat was made of wood overlaid in gold (Exodus 25:10-22). The Ark carried the following: Ten Commandments written on stones, some of the manna sealed in a jar that God gave the children of Israel to eat, and Aaron's Rod that still had blossoms on it although it was dead (Hebrews 9:4). God's Word, God's Provision, God's Miracles, Power, and Authority were all represented in this one Holy chest.

For three months, David had to leave the Ark in the home of Obededom, a man of God and Levite whose house the Lord blessed abundantly (2 Samuel 6:11, 12). So, when David was finally able to bring The Ark of God back to the place where it belonged, he danced and praised the Lord like he had lost his mind (2 Samuel 6:14)!

The Ark had not been in Jerusalem for 20 years prior to David taking the opportunity to bring it back. The Philistines had stolen the Ark, believing it would bring them some luck. They didn't realize that the God of Israel was a faithful God to His people.

They placed the Ark next to their gods in their temple, which was a huge mistake. Instead of the Ark bringing them good luck, it brought nothing but destruction and devastation (1 Samuel 5). If the Philistines had known Jehovah, they would have understood that they shouldn't have had any other gods before the One True and Living God (Exodus 20:3; Deuteronomy 5:7).

Everywhere the Presence of the Lord went in the enemies' camp, havoc ensued. So, they sent the Ark away with offerings of gold for repentance to a nearby Israeli town until King David was prompted to go after the Ark himself.

Reading this account in First and Second Samuel and First and Second Chronicles signifies the need for a true reverence for the things of God. Whenever anyone dishonored God's Presence, He broke out on them (2 Samuel 6:7)! So, with explicit precision, David worshipped, praised, and honored the Lord with sacrificial giving and brought God's Presence back to Jerusalem.

This is where 1 Chronicles 16 is developed, through David's heartfelt worship unto God. What will you do to invoke the Presence of the Lord in your life? What can you do to honor Him today? The children of Israel wavered back and forth in their relationship with God; therefore, His Presence was not always with them. They didn't always honor Him and consistently left Him to go after other things they set up as gods.

You and I have the privilege of always having God present with us all of the time. We can make the choice to invite Him into our daily experiences anytime. We don't have to carry a huge heavy box with us everywhere we go to have the Presence of the Lord in our midst. We can worship, praise, and honor Him anytime, allowing Him to have center stage in our lives.

Allow Jesus Christ to be the Center and the Circumference, the Base and the Boundary, the Beauty and the Balance of your everyday existence. You have the choice to always be in God's Holy Presence for He said He would never leave us nor forsake us (Hebrews 13:5). He'll be right here with us until the end of our days and far beyond.

My Notes

THIRTY

A Prayer of Faith and Declaration

May the blessings of divine grace and supernatural peace that flow from God our wonderful Father, and our Messiah, the Lord Jesus, be upon your lives.

I pray with great faith for you, because I'm fully convinced that the One who began this gracious work in you will faithfully continue the process of maturing you until the unveiling of our Lord Jesus Christ!

PHILIPPIANS 1:2, 6 TPT

God bless you today! As we complete this 31-day devotional, I pray that you have gotten a little closer to our Lord and Master Jesus Christ. Life is so much Better with Him than without Him. He is the Lifter of our heads and the Lover of our souls. I pray you share this devotional with others, and I also pray for you to start over again on day one because I believe you'll receive some new nuggets.

Paul, the Apostle of Christ, and his son in the faith Timothy composed this letter to the Philippian church while Paul may have been imprisoned. He began this letter with a prayer and a blessing. Can you imagine being in the worst position of your life and still having a heart and a desire to pronounce the blessing of the Lord on others? This is the epitome of the Christian Faith. It is the Heart of the Father and the Heart of His Dear Son, Jesus Christ.

Jesus' life for ours. That was the price, and that was the cost. So, we must live this life, giving it right back to Him—our life for His. Jesus paid the price for each one of us to live a faith-filled abundant life. This is why Paul pronounced this blessing because Jesus paid the ultimate price with His Life so that you and I can have the riches of Heaven.

I often wonder how someone in the deepest darkest of prison's pits can still have such joy. It's the same reason you and I can have joy during our most significant trials and tests. Joy must start on the inside. This joy is centered in receiving and getting to know Jesus more; this joy is where we draw our strength and what we need to rely on daily.

We have the blessing of Divine Grace so that we can handle every storm. And we have Supernatural Peace that keeps us rooted and grounded in the Father when the enemy tries to throw us off with his tricks and schemes. Finally, we have the knowledge that all these amazing things flow from our God, our Wonderful Father, and our Messiah, the Lord Jesus.

This Blessing of the Lord has been released into our lives. Regardless of our current circumstances, God's Hand is upon us for good. I'm going to declare it again. God's Hand is upon your life for good. You don't have to fight for the Blessing; all you must do is confess it and receive it with thanksgiving.

Again, I love what Paul prays for the people in the church in Philippi. This is also my prayer for you. He says, "I pray with great faith for you, because I'm fully convinced that the One who began this gracious work in you will faithfully continue the process of maturing you until the unveiling of our Lord Jesus Christ."

Maturity in Christ is the goal, and it's for our gain. It's how we win every battle, and it's why Paul was able to do amazing ministry from a prison cell. You, my dear child of the Most High God, are a winner; you are victorious. So, I pray you would increase your maturity in Christ, allowing God to perfect you in every storm. And once we are strengthened, we can bring strength to others also!

My Notes

THIRTY-ONE

And One More Thing

So now there is no condemnation for those who belong to Christ Jesus. And because you belong to him, the power of the life-giving Spirit has freed you from the power of sin that leads to death.

Romans 8:1-2 NLT

May the Word of God abide in you richly that you may receive victory every day and in every way. We know the wicked one desires to defeat us on every side, but with the Weapon of the Word of God, we win. May God's Amazing Word shape you and sharpen you to walk as strong believers in Christ. May you know beyond a shadow of a doubt that you are much more than you ever imagined and greater than you ever expected because the Greater One lives in you. You can't be defeated! You're not defeated; you will always win with God as your Guide!

Psalm 23:3 in the New Living Translation announces, "He (my Heavenly Father) renews my strength. He guides me along right paths, bringing honor to his name." Make this pronouncement over your life every day before you get on your way, earmarking what you expect each day to bring to you. Your expectation from the Lord should always be to receive His Strength and Guidance for direction to take the right paths for your life. Then, when you make good decisions by taking the right path, others will see it and Glorify your God. It gives you an open door to share your faith in following your Heavenly Father.

The Word of God states in the King James Version that we are to keep God's Word as frontlets between our eyes (Exodus 13:16; Deuteronomy 6:8 and 11:18). In the Hebrew custom, which is still practiced today, the devout Jewish men and sometimes even women would tie a band around their heads with a small leather box containing Scriptures inside when they attend prayers. It is a natural reminder to keep the Word of God-centered in your mind and always between your eyes. By reading it daily, we as Christians make this a practice as well to keep the Word of God at the forefront of our lives.

God's Word has to be our priority. This means taking devoted time each day to read, hear and comprehend the Scriptures so we can stand strong through any circumstance that may come our way, which is the primary purpose for devotionals like the one you have in your hands right now!

As I previously stated, you will win, and you are winning! It may seem like, at times, you are bruised, battered, and beaten down, but you will rise from the low places that come against your life! God's Promise is sure. Keep the Word first, and read other authorized translations of the Bible to better understand your here and now. God's Word is timeless. The Word of God is an eternal book and an internal book. The Word never gets old; we must allow it to work in and through us before it can work for us.

Your transformation is God's Priority. I hope you continue to let the Holy Scriptures soften your heart to receive more of Him. To learn and receive more of the One Who resides in Heaven and desires to have an integral part of your earthly everyday experience describes the Christian journey. As you devour this devotional in the coming months, I pray that you will continue to be *Excessively Blessed.*

My Notes

About the Author

Dr. Halene Marie Giddens is the First Lady of Destiny Christian Center, located in Victorville, California. She and her husband, Bishop Jesse Giddens, have been married for over 35 years. The two of them have been in full-time ministry together over 27 years. They have two adult children, Brittney Halene Marie and Jonathan David.

Dr. Halene is a licensed and ordained minister of the Gospel. She received her bachelor's degree in Biblical Studies from Speak the Word School of Ministry in 1996, her Master's Degree in Theology from the Institute of Teaching God's Word in 1998, and her Doctorate of Ministry from the Minnesota Graduate School of Theology in 2005. She, along with her husband, Bishop Giddens, completed the Sonship School of the Firstborn under the tutelage of the late Apostle Nathaniel Holcomb, who recently transitioned to be with the Lord, and their spiritual mother, Pastor Valerie Ivy Holcomb in 2007.

She is a sought-after speaker at women's conferences, seminars, and churches. She is anointed and has been appointed to speak the Word in due season to them that are weary. Dr. Halene also established the Women With Destiny (WWD) and Daughters of Destiny Ministries, where both are geared toward Christian women's spiritual health and development.

She says, "It is a privilege and honor to be able to share the life-changing Word of God with God's people." Most importantly, she truly loves the One she preaches about, Who is Jesus Christ, the Son of the Living God.

Dr. Halene says of her life that she has learned to trust in the Lord her God and encourages others to seek and sustain an intimate walk with Christ. She enjoys being alongside her husband in ministry and wouldn't have it any other way.

Her Books

Be ignited in your heart and in your mind to do you— the you that's set aside for the Glory of God to be the very best you that you can possibly be! That's the goal, and that's the gain. You'll never be satisfied until you fulfill your God-given, God-designed, God-inspired purpose on this side of life! It's already in you to succeed and to win; you're pre-wired to do well. You've just got to tap into the well of God's goodness that He wants to pour out on you for success!

In this Excessively Blessed Devotional, *Pause in God's Presence.* Give your worries over to Him, letting the fear cease to taunt you and halting all doubt because you are in the presence of the Almighty. God is our present help and Sovereign Savior Who you can trust with your every concern and care. He holds your future in His hands. He is a Safe and Powerful Place in which we find refuge! As you *Pause in His Presence,* know that He is always present with you. Always!

Destiny Christian Center

For more information about Destiny Christian Center, speaking engagements, or additional resources, please contact us at:

14380 Amargosa Rd.
Victorville, California 92392
Phone 760-951-8500
www.destinychristiancenter.org

We look forward to hearing from you soon!

www.ingramcontent.com/pod-product-compliance
Lightning Source LLC
Chambersburg PA
CBHW051826090426
42736CB00011B/1676
* 9 7 8 1 7 3 2 1 2 7 7 4 6 *